Good Housekeeping Cookery Club

*I*NDIAN

Janet Smith

EBURY PRESS
LONDON

First published 1995

1 3 5 7 9 10 8 6 4 2

First published in the United Kingdom in 1995 by Ebury Press, Random House, 20 Vauxhall Bridge Road, London SW1V 2SA

Random House Australia (Pty) Limited
20 Alfred Street, Milsons Point, Sydney,
New South Wales 2061, Australia

Random House New Zealand Limited
18 Poland Road, Glenfield,
Auckland 10, New Zealand

Random House South Africa (Pty) Limited
PO Box 337, Bergvlei, South Africa

Random House UK Limited Reg. No. 954009

A CIP catalogue record for this book is available from the British Library.

Managing Editor: JANET ILLSLEY
Design: SARA KIDD
Special Photography: JAMES MURPHY
Food Stylist: JANET SMITH
Photographic Stylist: ROISIN NIELD
Techniques Photography: KARL ADAMSON
Food Techniques Stylist: ANGELA KINGSBURY
Recipe Testing: EMMA-LEE GOW

ISBN 0 09 180 786 7

Typeset in Gill Sans by Textype Typesetters, Cambridge
Colour Separations by Magnacraft, London
Printed and bound in Italy by New Interlitho Italia S.p.a., Milan

CONTENTS

COOKERY NOTES

- Both metric and imperial measures are given for the recipes. Follow either metric or imperial throughout as they are not interchangeable.
- All spoon measures are level unless otherwise stated. Sets of measuring spoons are available in metric and imperial for accurate measurements of small quantities.
- Ovens should be preheated to the specified temperature. Grills should also be preheated. The cooking times given in the recipes assume that this has been done.

- Where a stage is specified under freezing, the dish should be frozen at the end of that stage.
- Size 2 eggs should be used except where otherwise specified. Free-range eggs are recommended.
- Use freshly ground black pepper and sea salt unless otherwise specified.
- Use fresh rather than dried herbs unless dried herbs are suggested in the recipe.
- Stocks should be freshly made if possible. Alternatively buy ready-made stocks or good quality stock cubes.

INTRODUCTION

The next time you fancy a curry, rather than rush to the nearest Indian restaurant, why not make something at home instead? With the increased availability of ingredients like fresh coriander, ginger and spices, Indian cooking is easy and rewarding.

In this book you'll find ideas for all occasions from quick, throw-together suppers to more time-consuming dishes for special occasions. Don't be fooled into thinking that all curries taste the same. Banish the memory of those old-fashioned curries that were nothing more than a meat stew overpoweringly flavoured with curry powder, sultanas and apples. Here we are talking rich, complex flavours – some subtle, others more powerful.

Remember, too, that spicy does not necessarily equal hot. It is chillies, either fresh or dried, or chilli powder, that add the heat to curries. If you look in shops and markets you will find that even in this country there is a wide range of chillies to choose from. Although generally the larger the chilli the milder the flavour, there are some dramatic exceptions. The only certain way to gauge potency is by taste. So when using an unidentified batch for the first time proceed with caution, adding a little at a time. For a milder dish, remove the seeds.

On a practical note, remember that chillies can 'burn'. If you're preparing several, do wear rubber gloves to protect your skin. If you're only using one or two chillies then this may be too much of an inconvenience, but do make sure that you wash your hands thoroughly afterwards.

If you're planning to cook a whole Indian meal, a few items of kitchen equipment will prove invaluable. A food processor or blender is almost essential for making curry pastes, and for puréeing onions, ginger and garlic. So too is a good, heavy pestle and mortar, or an electric spice grinder: home-crushed and roasted spices taste much fresher than anything you can buy, and grinding them yourself is part of the charm of Indian cookery. In an emergency, you could use a strong bowl and a rolling pin, but this is much less poetic and accidents are bound to happen!

I also find a good roomy, heavy-based flameproof casserole dish (such as le Cruset) most useful. A wok or flat-based metal karai pan is helpful too, for frying bhajis, poppadums and pakoras.

MENU PLANNING

Traditional Indian meals do not follow the usual course-by-course pattern. Instead, a selection of dishes is served at once: usually a meat or fish dish, a vegetable dish with bread and/or rice, and perhaps a dal, as well as a selection of chutneys and yogurt or raita. For vegetarians, an extra pulse, dal or vegetable dish is served instead of meat or fish. Fresh fruit normally rounds off the meal, but on special occasions a dessert is served.

For convenience, a chapter of snacks and starters is included in this book. These are intended to be eaten as a light meal or snack perhaps with raita and a salad, or they can be served as part of the main course, or as a starter on their own. Alternatively, they make interesting party food.

When planning your Indian menu, think in terms of dry and wet dishes, hot and sour, spicy and subtle, as well as hot and mild. Aim to serve a variety of dishes balanced for flavour and texture as well as colour. The menu suggestions overleaf may help you with your choice.

Don't forget that the shops offer a selection of ready-prepared items for supplementing your homemade curries. Many of these are good, but some taste of raw spices and are disappointing. On the whole, I would stick to shop-bought naan breads, chapatis, chutneys, samosas and bhajis, and make your own fresh-tasting accompaniments (see pages 7-9).

Samosas

Homemade samosas are much tastier than any you can buy and they are easy to make. Serve them with raita and a chutney. A crisp salad is also a good accompaniment. For convenience, these samosas can be made in advance and later reheated in the oven at 180°C (350°F) Mark 4 for about 15 minutes.

MAKES 12

FILLING
1 potato
1 onion
1 garlic clove
2.5 cm (1 inch) piece fresh
    root ginger
30 ml (2 tbsp) vegetable oil
5 ml (1 tsp) chilli powder
10 ml (2 tsp) ground
    coriander
10 ml (2 tsp) ground cumin
large pinch of grated nutmeg
large pinch of ground cloves
225 g (8 oz) lean minced
    lamb
handful of spinach leaves
30 ml (2 tbsp) each chopped
    fresh coriander and mint
salt and pepper

PASTRY
450 g (1 lb) plain white flour
5 ml (1 tsp) salt
5 ml (1 tsp) cumin seeds
60 ml (4 tbsp) vegetable oil,
    melted ghee or butter

TO FINISH
oil for deep-frying

PREPARATION TIME
45 minutes
COOKING TIME
10 minutes
FREEZING Suitable

310 CALS PER SAMOSA

1. Peel and finely chop the potato and onion. Skin and crush the garlic. Peel and finely chop the ginger. Heat the oil in a frying pan. Add the potato, onion and garlic and cook for about 5 minutes until the potato is softened.

2. Add the spices and cook, stirring, for 2 minutes. Add the minced lamb and cook for about 5 minutes until browned, stirring all the time. Add 30 ml (2 tbsp) water, lower the heat, cover and simmer for about 20 minutes or until the lamb and potato are tender. The mixture should be fairly dry; boil rapidly if necessary to reduce excess liquid.

3. Trim and chop the spinach leaves. Add to the pan and cook for about 1 minute, until just wilted. Add the chopped herbs and plenty of seasoning. Remove from the heat and leave to cool.

4. To make the pastry, mix together the flour, salt and cumin seeds in a bowl. Mix in the oil or melted fat and about 200 ml (7 fl oz) warm water to make a soft dough. Turn onto a lightly floured surface and knead for about 5 minutes.

5. Divide the dough into 12 even pieces; keep covered with a damp cloth to prevent them drying out. Take one piece and roll out to a circle, about 15 cm (6 inches) in diameter. Use a small plate as a guide to neaten the edges if liked. Cut in half to make two semi-circles.

6. Put a heaped teaspoonful of filling on each semi-circle. Dampen the edges, then fold over the filling and press together firmly with your fingers to seal. Repeat with the remaining pastry and filling.

7. Heat the oil in a deep-fat fryer. Test the temperature by dropping in a small piece of pastry – it should sizzle immediately on contact with the oil and rise to the surface; remove with a slotted spoon.

8. Deep-fry the samosas 2 or 3 at a time for about 3-5 minutes or until pale golden brown. Drain on crumpled kitchen paper and serve warm, garnished with lemon and lime wedges.

TECHNIQUE

Put a heaped teaspoonful of filling on each semi-circle of dough. Moisten the edges of the dough, then fold over the filling and press together to seal.

ONION BHAJIS

Gram flour gives these bhajis an authentic flavour. Also known as besan, it is a very fine-textured flour made from ground chick peas. Gram flour is available from Indian grocers and food emporiums, but if you are unable to find it, plain wholemeal flour makes a good substitute. Bhajis can be prepared in advance and reheated on a baking sheet at 200°C (400°F) Mark 6 for about 10 minutes before serving.

MAKES 12

450 g (1 lb) onions

1 garlic clove

2.5 cm (1 inch) piece fresh
   root ginger

1-2 hot red chillies

5 ml (1 tsp) ground
   turmeric

5 ml (1 tsp) ground
   cardamom seeds (see
   note)

125 g (4 oz) gram or plain
   wholemeal flour, sifted

50 g (2 oz) white self-raising
   flour

45 ml (3 tbsp) chopped fresh
   mint

salt and pepper

15 ml (1 tbsp) lemon juice

oil for deep-frying

TO GARNISH

mint sprigs

lime wedges

PREPARATION TIME
20 minutes
COOKING TIME
10 minutes
FREEZING
Suitable

180 CALS PER BHAJI

1. Peel and halve the onions. Cut each half into very thin crescent-shaped slices. Peel and finely chop the garlic and ginger. Finely chop the chillies, discarding the seeds if a milder flavour is preferred.

2. Put the onions, garlic, ginger and chillies in a bowl. Add the spices and toss well. Add the flours, mint and salt and pepper. Mix thoroughly.

3. Add the lemon juice and about 75 ml (5 tbsp) cold water or enough to make the mixture cling together; do not make it too wet.

4. Heat the oil in a deep-fat fryer. Test the temperature by dropping in a small piece of bread – it should sizzle immediately on contact with the oil and rise to the surface; remove with a slotted spoon.

5. Meanwhile divide the mixture into 12 even portions. Using dampened hands, shape each portion into a ball. Pat firmly to ensure that it will hold together during cooking, but don't worry if it doesn't form a neat round.

6. Deep-fry 3-4 bhajis at a time in the hot oil for 5 minutes or until golden brown on all sides. Carefully remove from the hot oil and drain on crumpled kitchen paper. Serve warm, garnished with mint sprigs and lime wedges.

NOTE: The crushed seeds from 12 cardamom pods will yield this quantity.

TECHNIQUE

Pat the onion balls firmly together to adhere, otherwise they may break up during cooking.

SEEKH KEBABS

Minced lamb is traditionally used for these kebabs, but you could use beef if you prefer. As a starter, they look most attractive served on a bed of fresh baby spinach leaves – tossed with a few chopped chillies and shredded red pepper or a few cherry tomatoes. Accompany with poppadums or chapatis.

MAKES 12-16

1 small onion
2 garlic cloves
2.5 cm (1 inch) piece fresh
    root ginger
1 hot red chilli
10 ml (2 tsp) coriander
    seeds
5 ml (1 tsp) ground
    fenugreek
5 ml (1 tsp) garam masala
5 ml (1 tsp) ground
    turmeric
15 ml (1 tbsp) ghee or
    vegetable oil, plus extra
    for brushing
450 g (1 lb) minced lamb
45 ml (3 tbsp) chopped fresh
    coriander
45 ml (3 tbsp) chopped fresh
    mint
salt and pepper
1 egg (size 3), beaten
TO SERVE
mint sprigs
shredded coriander or chilli
lemon wedges

PREPARATION TIME
20 minutes
COOKING TIME
10 minutes
FREEZING
Not suitable

95-70 CALS PER KEBAB

1. Peel and quarter the onion. Peel the garlic and ginger. Chop the chilli, discarding the seeds if a milder flavour is preferred. Put these ingredients into a blender or food processor and process until finely chopped.

2. Crush the coriander seeds with a pestle and mortar and add to the onion paste with the remaining spices. Process until evenly blended.

3. Heat 15 ml (1 tbsp) ghee or oil in a frying pan and add the onion paste. Cook over a medium heat for 2-3 minutes, stirring all the time. Remove from the heat and allow to cool.

4. Put the minced lamb in a bowl and break it up with a fork. Add the chopped coriander and mint and season with salt and pepper. Add the cooled onion paste and mix thoroughly. Add just enough of the beaten egg to bind; don't add too much or you will make the mixture too wet to shape.

5. Divide the mixture into 12-16 portions. Using floured hands, shape each portion into a flattened sausage around one end of a bamboo skewer. Press the mixture firmly so that it sticks together. Repeat to make about 12-16 kebabs.

6. Brush the kebabs with melted ghee or oil. Cook under a very hot grill for about 10 minutes or until browned on the outside and cooked right through, turning the kebabs as they cook to ensure that they brown evenly. Serve garnished with mint and shredded coriander or chilli. Accompany with lemon wedges.

NOTE: If your grill pan is small, you may need to cook the kebabs in two batches. To prevent scorching during grilling, presoak the bamboo skewers in water for about 10 minutes.

VARIATION

Rather than shape the mixture into kebabs around bamboo skewers, simply form into balls or patties and shallow-fry or grill until evenly browned and cooked through.

TECHNIQUE

Using floured hands, mould each portion around one end of a bamboo skewer to form a flattened sausage.

KOFTAS

These make a great lunchtime snack, served with raita and shop-bought naan. If serving as a starter, scatter the onion relish over them and accompany with poppadums or chapatis. Alternatively, shape bite-size koftas to serve as party food; make them well in advance of the party, freeze and reheat on the day.

MAKES 24

KOFTAS
1 small onion
1 garlic clove
2.5 cm (1 inch) piece fresh
   root ginger
5 ml (1 tsp) ground cumin
5 ml (1 tsp) ground
   coriander
45 ml (3 tbsp) ghee or
   vegetable oil
450 g (1 lb) minced beef
45 ml (3 tbsp) chopped fresh
   coriander
salt and pepper
1 egg (size 3)

ONION RELISH
1 red onion
45 ml (3 tbsp) chopped or
   roughly torn fresh
   coriander
1 lime
1 large red chilli (optional)
1 garlic clove

PREPARATION TIME
20 minutes
COOKING TIME
10 minutes
FREEZING
Suitable

40 CALS PER KOFTA

1. First make the onion relish. Peel and quarter the onion, then slice thinly. Put into a bowl with the chopped coriander. Grate the lime rind into the bowl. Finely slice the chilli, if using, discarding the seeds if a milder flavour is preferred. Peel and chop the garlic. Add the chilli and garlic to the onion relish with a squeeze of lime juice. Toss to mix, then set aside while making the koftas.

2. To make the koftas, peel and quarter the onion; peel the garlic; peel and halve the ginger. Put these ingredients in a blender or food processor and work until finely chopped. Add the spices and process until evenly mixed.

3. Heat 15 ml (1 tbsp) of the ghee or oil in a frying pan and add the onion paste. Cook over a medium heat for 2-3 minutes, stirring all the time. Remove from the heat and allow to cool.

4. Put the minced beef in a bowl and break it up with a fork. Add the chopped coriander and season with salt and pepper. Add the cooled onion paste and mix thoroughly until evenly incorporated. Add just sufficient beaten egg to bind; don't add too much or the mixture will be too sticky to shape.

5. Using lightly floured hands, shape the spiced beef mixture into approximately 24 small balls.

6. Heat the remaining ghee or oil in the frying pan and add the koftas. Cook for about 5 minutes or until browned on all sides and cooked right through, shaking the pan as they cook to ensure they brown evenly. Drain the koftas on kitchen paper. Serve hot, with the onion relish and raita.

NOTE: If your frying pan is small you may need to cook the koftas in 2-3 batches.

TECHNIQUE

With lightly floured hands, shape the mixture into 24 small balls.

MUSSELS IN SPICED COCONUT MILK

Mussels are often served in a creamy coconut sauce in the southern Indian state of Goa. If you are not keen on mussels, you can make an equally delicious dish, using prawns instead (see variation).

SERVES 3-4

1.8 kg (4 lb) fresh mussels in shells
5 ml (1 tsp) fenugreek seeds
10 ml (2 tsp) cumin seeds
10 ml (2 tsp) coriander seeds
2 medium onions
4 garlic cloves
2.5 cm (1 inch) piece fresh root ginger
30 ml (2 tbsp) ghee or vegetable oil
4 cloves
1 cinnamon stick
3 dried red chillies
4 curry leaves (optional)
45 ml (3 tbsp) lime or lemon juice
600 ml (1 pint) coconut milk
salt
TO GARNISH
30 ml (2 tbsp) sesame seeds
coarsely grated fresh coconut (optional)

PREPARATION TIME
20 minutes
COOKING TIME
10 minutes
FREEZING
Not suitable

630-475 CALS PER SERVING

1. To prepare the mussels, scrub thoroughly under cold running water, scraping off any barnacles or seaweed. Pull or cut off the hairy 'beard' protruding from the shell. Discard any mussels with cracked or broken shells, or any that refuse to close when tapped with the back of the knife. Put the mussels in a colander and set aside while making the sauce.

2. Dry-fry the fenugreek, cumin and coriander seeds in a small heavy-based pan until they begin to release their aroma, shaking the pan frequently so they do not burn. Allow to cool, then crush using a pestle and mortar.

3. Peel and quarter the onions. Peel the garlic. Peel and halve the ginger. Put the onions, garlic and ginger in a blender or food processor with the dry-fried spices. Purée until smooth, adding a little water if necessary to prevent sticking.

4. Heat the ghee or oil in a large heavy-based saucepan or flameproof casserole. Add the onion mixture and fry for about 5 minutes until browned, stirring all the time. Add the cloves, cinnamon, chillies and curry leaves and fry for 2 minutes.

5. Add the lime or lemon juice, coconut milk, salt and 150 ml (¼ pint) water. Bring to the boil, lower heat and simmer for 5 minutes, stirring occasionally.

6. Add the mussels, cover with a tight-fitting lid and cook, shaking the pan occasionally, for 5 minutes or until the mussels have opened. Discard any that do not open.

7. Serve in warmed bowls, sprinkled with sesame seeds and coconut if desired.

VARIATION

Replace the mussels with 700 g (1½ lb) medium raw prawns in their shells and prepare according to the instructions in the following recipe (page 22). Alternatively use 450 g (1 lb) large cooked peeled prawns, heating through for 1-2 minutes only.

TECHNIQUE

Scrub the mussels thoroughly under cold running water, scraping off any barnacles or seaweed with a small sharp knife.

PRAWNS FRIED WITH OKRA

Otherwise known as bindi or ladies' fingers, okra are used extensively in Indian cookery. When trimming okra, snip only a tiny piece from each end. Avoid cutting into the flesh or the okra will become sticky and soggy during cooking. This dish is most successful when cooked in a wok, rather like a stir-fry; if using a frying pan make sure that it is a large one.

SERVES 4

700 g (1½ lb) raw prawns in shells (see note)
450 g (1 lb) fresh okra
2 medium onions (preferably red)
2 small green chillies
1 garlic clove (optional)
3 medium ripe juicy tomatoes
45 ml (3 tbsp) ghee or vegetable oil
10 ml (2 tsp) ground cumin
15 ml (1 tbsp) mustard seeds
salt and pepper
squeeze of lemon juice, to taste
10 ml (2 tsp) garam masala
45 ml (3 tbsp) coarsely grated fresh coconut or desiccated coconut, toasted if preferred

PREPARATION TIME
25 minutes
COOKING TIME
10 minutes
FREEZING
Not suitable

300 CALS PER SERVING

1. Remove the heads from the prawns if necessary, then shell, leaving the tail end attached. Using a small sharp knife, make a shallow slit along the outer curve from the tail end to the head end and remove the dark intestinal vein (see technique, page 24). Rinse the prawns under cold running water. Drain and pat dry with kitchen paper.

2. Wash and trim the okra. Peel the onions and cut into thin rings. Slice the chillies, discarding the seeds if a milder flavour is preferred. Peel and slice the garlic, if using. Cut the tomatoes into small wedges.

3. Heat the ghee or oil in a wok or large heavy-based frying pan. Add the onions and cook over a high heat until browned. Add the okra, prawns, chillies, garlic if using, cumin and mustard seeds. Cook over a high heat, shaking the pan constantly, for 5 minutes or until the prawns are bright pink and the okra is softened but not soggy.

4. Add the tomato wedges and salt and pepper to taste. Cook for 1-2 minutes to heat through; the tomatoes should retain their shape. Add a little lemon juice, to taste.

5. Turn the mixture into a serving dish and sprinkle with the garam masala and coconut. Serve immediately.

NOTE: If raw prawns in shells are unobtainable, substitute 450 g (1 lb) cooked shelled prawns, choosing the largest ones available. Add with the tomatoes in step 5 and heat through only; do not overcook or they will be tough.

TECHNIQUE

Remove the heads from the prawns and peel away the shells, leaving the fan-like tail shell attached.

PRAWNS WITH SPINACH

Fresh spinach gives this dish a wonderful vibrance that you simply won't obtain with the frozen alternative. Look for packs of ready-washed and trimmed spinach leaves, which are now widely available from most of the larger supermarkets. Similarly raw prawns are now sold by supermarkets as well as fishmongers. For optimum flavour do use them if possible – in preference to cooked prawns.

SERVES 4

700 g (1½ lb) large raw
   prawns in shells (see note)
1 medium onion
1 garlic clove
5 cm (2 inch) piece fresh
   root ginger
450 g (1 lb) spinach leaves
30 ml (2 tbsp) ghee or
   vegetable oil
10 ml (2 tsp) ground
   turmeric
5 ml (1 tsp) chilli powder
15 ml (1 tbsp) black
   mustard seeds
10 ml (2 tsp) ground
   coriander
large pinch of ground cloves
300 ml (½ pint) coconut
   milk
salt
15 ml (1 tbsp) lime or lemon
   juice

PREPARATION TIME
25 minutes
COOKING TIME
15 minutes
FREEZING
Not suitable

255 CALS PER SERVING

1. To prepare the raw prawns, remove the heads, if necessary, then peel off the shell leaving the fan-like piece at the end of the tail attached (see technique, page 22). Using a small sharp knife, make a shallow slit along the back of each prawn and remove the dark intestinal vein. Rinse the prawns under cold running water. Drain and pat dry with kitchen paper.

2. Peel and slice the onion. Peel and chop the garlic. Peel the ginger and cut into thin strips.

3. Trim the spinach leaves and wash thoroughly in several changes of water if necessary; drain well.

4. Heat the ghee or oil in a large frying pan or wok. Add the onion, garlic and ginger and fry, stirring, until softened. Add the spices and cook for 2 minutes, stirring all the time.

5. Add the coconut milk, bring to the boil, then lower the heat and simmer for 5 minutes. Add the prawns and simmer for about 4 minutes or until they just begin to look opaque.

6. Add the spinach; it may be difficult to fit it all in but don't worry, it will reduce down as it cooks in the steam. Cover the pan with a lid or a baking tray and cook for about 3 minutes or until the spinach is wilted; don't keep removing the lid to check during cooking or you will let the steam escape.

7. Stir the wilted spinach into the sauce and add the lime or lemon juice. Serve immediately.

NOTE: If raw prawns are unobtainable, substitute 450 g (1 lb) cooked shelled prawns choosing the largest ones available. Add to the pan 1-2 minutes before the end of the cooking time, to heat through only.

TECHNIQUE

Using a small sharp knife, make a shallow slit along the outer curve of each prawn from the tail to the head end and remove the dark intestinal vein.

FISH MASALA

The rich spicy sauce in this recipe complements most white fish. I prefer to use fish steaks or fillets because they are easiest to eat with a sauce like this, but you could pour it over small whole fish. Coating the fish with flour and frying it before mixing with the sauce isn't authentic, but I prefer the resulting texture and appearance. However, if you want to save time, effort and calories, simply omit step 5.

SERVES 4

5 large juicy tomatoes
1 medium onion
2 garlic cloves
1-2 hot green chillies
2.5 cm (1 inch) piece fresh
   root ginger
60 ml (4 tbsp) chopped fresh
   coriander
juice of 2 limes
15 ml (1 tbsp) coriander
   seeds
5 ml (1 tsp) fenugreek seeds
5 ml (1 tsp) ground
   turmeric
30 ml (2 tbsp) vegetable oil
15 ml (1 tbsp) garam masala
salt
4 white fish steaks, such as
   cod, haddock, halibut
about 30 ml (2 tbsp) plain
   white flour, for coating
oil for shallow-frying

PREPARATION TIME
15 minutes
COOKING TIME
20 minutes
FREEZING
Suitable: Sauce only

360 CALS PER SERVING

1. Immerse the tomatoes in boiling water for 30 seconds, then drain and peel away the skins. Finely chop the tomatoes. Peel and quarter the onion. Peel the garlic. Halve the chillies, discarding the seeds if a milder flavour is preferred. Peel and halve the ginger.

2. Put the onion, garlic, chillies, ginger, chopped coriander and lime juice in a blender or food processor and process to make a fairly thick paste.

3. Crush the coriander and fenugreek seeds using a pestle and mortar, then add to the spice paste with the turmeric and mix well.

4. Heat the oil in a large frying pan. Add the spice paste and cook, stirring constantly, for about 5 minutes. Stir in the chopped tomatoes, garam masala and salt to taste. Cook for about 5 minutes or until the tomatoes have broken down and their liquid has evaporated.

5. Coat the fish steaks with the flour. Heat the oil in another frying pan. Add the fish steaks and quickly brown on both sides.

6. Transfer the fish steaks to the frying pan containing the sauce, arranging them in a single layer. Spoon a little of the sauce over each fish steak and cover the pan with a lid or a baking sheet. Simmer

gently for about 8-10 minutes, depending on the thickness of the fish, until the fish is cooked right through. Serve at once, with plenty of boiled rice to mop up the sauce.

TECHNIQUE

Crush the coriander and fenugreek seeds using a pestle and mortar.

SPICED FRIED FISH

The fish eaten in India is different from the fish we can obtain here. For this dish you will need firm fillets that won't break up during cooking. Firm-textured monkfish is the best choice but it is quite expensive. Although a little more delicate, cod and haddock fillet – cut from the thickest part of the fish – also work well. Serve the spiced fish with a rice dish and raita or chutney.

SERVES 4

700 g (1½ lb) firm white fish fillets

1-2 hot red chillies

1 bunch of fresh coriander

1 garlic clove

10 ml (2 tsp) plain white flour

large pinch of salt

5 ml (1 tsp) cumin seeds

10 ml (2 tsp) coriander seeds

1 lime

oil for shallow-frying

lime wedges, to garnish

PREPARATION TIME
20 minutes
COOKING TIME
10 minutes
FREEZING
Not suitable

285 CALS PER SERVING

1. Skin the fish fillets and cut into large chunks. Chop the chillies, discarding the seeds if a milder flavour is preferred. Trim the roots (if still attached) and most of the tough stems from the coriander, then finely chop the leaves. Peel the garlic and chop very finely.

2. Put the coriander, chillies and garlic in a large bowl and mix with the flour and salt.

3. Heat a small heavy-based frying pan. Add the cumin and coriander seeds and dry-fry for 2 minutes, stirring all the time so that they do not burn. Allow to cool, then finely crush the spices using a pestle and mortar. Add them to the flour mixture.

4. Using a fine grater, grate the rind from the lime directly into the bowl.

5. Add the prepared fish to the spiced flour mixture and toss carefully to ensure that each piece is coated on all sides.

6. Heat the oil in a frying pan. Cook the fish, a few pieces at a time, until browned and crisp on the outside and cooked right through. Drain on kitchen paper and keep warm while cooking the rest of the fish. Serve at once, garnished with lime wedges.

TECHNIQUE

Using your hands, carefully toss the chunks of fish in the spiced flour to coat thoroughly.

CARDAMOM CHICKEN WITH PEPPERS

This spiced whole roast chicken makes a pleasant change from the usual Sunday roast. Extract the tiny seeds from cardamom pods a day ahead if you are likely to be short of time on the day.

SERVES 4

1 roasting chicken, about 1.4 kg (3 lb)
5 ml (1 tsp) ground turmeric
salt
3 garlic cloves
1 red chilli
2.5 cm (1 inch) piece fresh root ginger
5 ml (1 tsp) fennel seeds
4 black peppercorns
seeds from 8 green cardamoms
150 ml (¼ pint) yogurt
3 medium onions
2 large red, yellow or orange peppers
45 ml (3 tbsp) ghee or vegetable oil
1 cinnamon stick
4 cloves
3 whole green cardamoms
2.5 ml (½ tsp) saffron strands
coriander sprigs, to garnish

PREPARATION TIME
20 minutes, plus marinating
COOKING TIME
About 1 hour 20 minutes
FREEZING
Not suitable

380 CALS PER SERVING

1. Make a note of the weight of the chicken and calculate the cooking time, allowing 20 minutes per 450 g (1 lb), plus 20 minutes. Mix the turmeric with 5 ml (1 tsp) salt and rub all over the chicken.

2. Peel and halve the garlic. Chop the chilli, discarding the seeds if a milder flavour is preferred. Peel the ginger and roughly chop. Put these ingredients in a blender or food processor, with the fennel seeds, peppercorns and cardamom seeds. Process until finely chopped, then add the yogurt and salt to taste and process again until evenly blended.

3. Coat the chicken with the spiced yogurt mixture and leave to marinate at cool room temperature for 1 hour, or in the refrigerator overnight.

4. Preheat the oven to 200°C (400°F) Mark 6. Peel and finely chop the onions. Halve, core and deseed the peppers, then cut the flesh into very thin strips.

5. Heat the ghee or oil in a flameproof casserole (large enough to hold the chicken). Add the cinnamon, cloves and cardamoms and fry for 2 minutes. Add the onions and cook for 10 minutes, stirring frequently, until soft and golden brown. Add the saffron and 300 ml (½ pint) boiling water. Bring to the boil, lower heat and simmer for 2 minutes.

6. Add the chicken with any yogurt mixture. Cover with a lid and cook in the oven for half the calculated time.

7. Add the peppers to the casserole. If most of the water has evaporated, add a little extra boiling water so that the peppers do not burn. Cook, uncovered, for the rest of the calculated time or until the chicken is cooked through and browned.

8. To serve, spoon the pepper and onion mixture onto a warmed platter. Put the chicken on top and moisten with a little of the cooking liquid. Garnish with coriander and serve immediately.

VARIATION

Use a jointed chicken or chicken pieces. Cook covered for 25 minutes, then uncovered for about 20 minutes.

TECHNIQUE

Coat chicken with the yogurt mixture.

CHICKEN DHANSAK

This north Indian combination of chicken and lentils is often made with three types of dal. I've simplified things somewhat by using masoor dal, better known as the common red split lentil, and chana dal which is available from larger supermarkets, wholefood stores and Indian grocers.

SERVES 6

6 chicken quarters
3 tomatoes
3 onions
6 garlic cloves
2.5 cm (1 inch) piece fresh
   root ginger
2-3 red chillies
15 ml (1 tbsp) coriander
   seeds
15 ml (1 tbsp) cumin seeds
5 black peppercorns
seeds from 4 cardamoms
10 ml (2 tsp) ground
   turmeric
10 ml (2 tsp) ground
   cinnamon
45 ml (3 tbsp) ghee or
   vegetable oil
175 g (6 oz) masoor dal (red
   split lentils)
175 g (6 oz) chana dal
5 ml (1 tsp) salt
3 small thin aubergines, or
   1 medium one
15 ml (1 tbsp) dark brown
   sugar
30 ml (2 tbsp) lemon juice

PREPARATION TIME
20 minutes
COOKING TIME
1 hour
FREEZING
Suitable

445 CALS PER SERVING

1. Skin the chicken quarters and cut each one into 2 or 3 pieces. Immerse the tomatoes in boiling water for 30 seconds, then drain and peel away the skins. Finely chop the tomatoes.

2. Peel and quarter the onions. Peel and halve the garlic. Peel and roughly chop the ginger. Chop the chillies, discarding the seeds if a milder flavour is preferred.

3. Put the onions, garlic, ginger and chillies in a food processor or blender with about 30 ml (2 tbsp) water. Process until very finely chopped. Add the spices and process again.

4. Heat the ghee or oil in a large heavy-based casserole. Add the spice paste and cook over a medium heat, stirring frequently, for about 10 minutes or until the onion is softened and golden brown. Add the chicken, increase the heat and cook, turning, for a couple of minutes until it is sealed on all sides.

5. Add the dals with the tomatoes and cook for 2 minutes, stirring all the time. Add enough water to just cover the dal and chicken and bring to the boil. Lower the heat, add the salt, cover and simmer for 20 minutes.

6. Halve the small aubergines (or cut the medium one into large chunks). Add to the dhansak with the sugar and lemon juice. Re-cover and simmer for a further 20-30 minutes or until the chicken is tender and the lentils are mushy. Check from time to time to make sure that the dhansak is not sticking and burning on the base of the pan. If it seems too dry add a little extra water. If the sauce is too thin once the chicken is cooked, reduce by boiling rapidly, uncovered, for a few minutes.

7. Using a potato masher or the back of a wooden spoon, mash the dals to break them down slightly. Check the seasoning, adding a little extra salt if necessary, before serving.

TECHNIQUE

Process the onions, garlic, ginger and chillies with 30 ml (2 tbsp) water until very finely chopped, then add the spices and process again.

CHICKEN KORMA

This universally popular chicken dish should be mild, rich and creamy, but not in any way bland. For best results, use a good thick yogurt; rich Greek-style yogurt is ideal. Don't be tempted to use a low-fat yogurt, as this would curdle and make the sauce unappetising. Serve the korma with plenty of rice or Indian bread to mop up the ample sauce.

SERVES 4

3 large onions, peeled

30-45 ml (2-3 tbsp) ghee or
   vegetable oil

2-3 garlic cloves

4 cloves

4 cardamom pods

1 cinnamon stick

10 ml (2 tsp) ground
   coriander

2.5 ml (½ tsp) ground
   turmeric

2.5 ml (½ tsp) ground ginger

2.5 ml (½ tsp) ground cumin

4 chicken breast fillets,
   skinned

squeeze of lemon juice

600 ml (1 pint) thick yogurt

salt

coriander sprigs, to garnish
   (optional)

PREPARATION TIME
15 minutes
COOKING TIME
40 minutes
FREEZING
Not suitable

390 CALS PER SERVING

1. Thinly slice half of the onions. Heat 30 ml (2 tbsp) ghee or oil in a frying pan, add the sliced onions and fry until browned and crisp. Remove with a slotted spoon and drain thoroughly on crumpled kitchen paper; set aside.

2. Finely chop the remaining onion. Peel and crush the garlic. Cook the onion and garlic in the ghee or oil remaining in the pan until softened, adding a little extra if necessary. Add the spices and cook, stirring constantly, for 2 minutes until the onions are lightly browned.

3. Cut each chicken breast fillet into 3 pieces. Add these to the pan with a squeeze of lemon juice and lower the heat. Add the yogurt, a tablespoon at a time, stirring thoroughly after each addition. Gradually stir in 150 ml (¼ pint) water.

4. Half-cover the pan with a lid and simmer gently for about 30 minutes until the chicken is tender and cooked right through. Season with salt to taste.

5. Serve sprinkled with the crisp browned onions, and garnished with coriander if desired.

VARIATION

Replace the chicken with 700 g (1½ lb) shelled large raw prawns or 450 g (1 lb) cooked peeled prawns. Add to the sauce in step 4. Cook for about 4 minutes if using raw prawns, until they turn pink. Cooked prawns only need to be heated through, for about 2 minutes.

TECHNIQUE

Add the chicken pieces to the onion, garlic and spice mixture in the pan, turning to coat them with the flavourings.

CHICKEN COOKED WITH WHOLE SPICES

Remind unsuspecting guests that the whole spices in this dish are not intended to be eaten! In Indian cooking it is usual to cook the chicken on the bone because it improves the flavour, but you could use chicken breast fillets if preferred (see variation).

SERVES 4

450 g (1 lb) onions
2-3 garlic cloves
**45 ml (3 tbsp) blanched
   almonds**
4 chicken quarters
**45-60 ml (3-4 tbsp) ghee or
   vegetable oil**
1 cinnamon stick
8 curry leaves
3 black cardamoms
4 cloves
4 black peppercorns
10 ml (2 tsp) cumin seeds
1-2 dried red chillies
**3 large ripe tomatoes,
   skinned if preferred**
salt

PREPARATION TIME
15 minutes
COOKING TIME
45 minutes
FREEZING
Suitable

445 CALS PER SERVING

1. Peel the onions and cut into wedges. Peel and chop the garlic. Finely chop the almonds. Halve each chicken quarter, discarding the skin.

2. Heat 45 ml (3 tbsp) ghee or oil in a large flameproof casserole or heavy-based pan. Add the onions and cook over a medium heat, stirring frequently, for 10-15 minutes until softened and golden brown. If they show signs of burning, add a little water to the pan.

3. Once the onions have browned, increase the heat to boil off any water if necessary. Add the whole spices and cook over a high heat for 2 minutes, stirring all the time. Add the almonds and cook for 1-2 minutes until they are lightly browned.

4. Remove the onions, almonds and spices from the pan, using a slotted spoon. Add a little extra ghee or oil to the pan if there is none remaining and heat until very hot. Add the chicken, a few pieces at a time, and cook over a high heat until browned on all sides. Remove the chicken pieces as they brown and set aside with the onions.

5. When all the pieces are browned, return all the chicken to the pan with the browned onions, almonds and spices.

6. Chop the tomatoes and add to the pan with 450 ml (¾ pint) water and salt to taste. Bring to the boil, then lower the heat. Cover and simmer for 45 minutes or until the chicken is very tender.

7. If the sauce is too thin once the chicken is cooked, transfer the chicken to a warmed serving dish and boil the sauce rapidly, uncovered, over a high heat for a few minutes until reduced. Pour the sauce over the chicken and serve immediately.

VARIATION

Use skinless chicken breast fillets rather than quarters. Cut each into 3 pieces and reduce the cooking time to 30 minutes.

TECHNIQUE

Add the whole spices to the browned onions and cook over a high heat for 2 minutes, stirring constantly.

TANDOORI-STYLE CHICKEN

At home the best way to emulate the intense direct heat of a tandoor oven is by grilling or barbecuing. It's essential to preheat the grill until very hot, and to keep the food fairly close to the heat source so that it gets well browned. Serve the tandoori chicken with a fresh-tasting Coriander Chutney (page 72).

SERVES 4

2-3 garlic cloves

2.5 cm (1 inch) piece fresh
    root ginger

1-2 hot green chillies

600 ml (1 pint) thick yogurt

15 ml (1 tbsp) ground
    coriander

15 ml (1 tbsp) ground cumin

10 ml (2 tsp) tandoori or
    curry paste

30 ml (2 tbsp) chopped fresh
    coriander

30 ml (2 tbsp) chopped fresh
    mint (optional)

salt

few drops each of red and
    yellow food colouring
    (optional)

8 chicken supremes, skinned

melted ghee, butter or oil,
    for basting

lemon or lime juice, to taste

lime or lemon wedges, to
    garnish

PREPARATION TIME
15 minutes, plus overnight
marinating
COOKING TIME
25 minutes
FREEZING
Not suitable

265 CALS PER SERVING

1. Peel and crush the garlic. Peel and finely chop the ginger. Chop the chillies, discarding the seeds if a milder flavour is preferred.

2. Put the yogurt in a large non-metallic dish and add the garlic, ginger and chillies. Add the ground spices and tandoori or curry paste and mix thoroughly. Add the chopped coriander and mint if using. Season with salt and add a few drops of food colouring to enhance the colour if desired.

3. Make 3-4 deep cuts in each chicken portion, being careful not to cut right through. Add the chicken to the marinade and turn to ensure that each piece is thoroughly coated. Rub the mixture well into the cuts. Cover the bowl and leave the chicken to marinate in the refrigerator overnight.

4. Preheat the grill (or barbecue) until it is very hot. Remove the chicken from the marinade and place on the grill (or barbecue) rack and cook for about 25 minutes, basting with melted ghee, butter or oil and turning frequently to ensure that it cooks evenly. Don't be afraid to let it get really brown in places; a few crusty crispy bits add to the flavour. To check that the chicken is cooked pierce the thickest part with

a skewer; the juices should run clear – if they are at all pink cook for longer.

5. Serve the tandoori chicken straight away, brushed with a little more melted ghee, butter or oil and sprinkled with lime or lemon juice. Serve garnished with lime or lemon wedges.

NOTE: If your grill pan is very small you may find it difficult to grill 8 chicken supremes, so either cook them in batches or bake in the oven at 200°C (400°F) Mark 6 for about 30 minutes.

TECHNIQUE

Turn the chicken pieces in the marinade and rub the mixture well into the cuts.

RED BEEF CURRY

As this curry cooks the liquid reduces, so that you are left with a rich, thick sauce clinging to the meat. It's important to use a casserole dish with a tight-fitting lid and to resist the temptation to keep lifting it during cooking, otherwise you will end up without any sauce and burnt meat! Serve this dish accompanied by a moist vegetable dish and a rice pilaf.

SERVES 4

2 onions
4 garlic cloves
1-2 red chillies (optional)
3 ripe juicy tomatoes
900 g (2 lb) stewing or
    braising steak
5 ml (1 tsp) black
    peppercorns
30 ml (2 tbsp) ghee or oil
15 ml (1 tbsp) paprika
5 ml (1 tsp) ground ginger
salt
300 ml (½ pint) thick yogurt

PREPARATION TIME
15 minutes
COOKING TIME
About 2 hours
FREEZING
Suitable

400 CALS PER SERVING

1. Preheat the oven to 170°C (325°F) Mark 3. Peel and finely chop the onions and garlic. Chop the chillies if using, discarding the seeds if a milder flavour is preferred.

2. Immerse the tomatoes in boiling water to cover, leave for about 1 minute, then remove and peel away the skins. Finely chop the tomato flesh.

3. Remove any excess fat from the meat, then cut into 4 cm (1½ inch) cubes. Crush the peppercorns, using a pestle and mortar.

4. Heat the ghee or oil in a large flameproof casserole. Quickly fry the meat in batches until thoroughly browned on all sides, then remove with a slotted spoon and set aside.

5. Add the onions and garlic to the casserole and cook, stirring, over a high heat for about 2 minutes. Lower the heat and cook until the onions are lightly browned.

6. Return all the meat to the casserole along with any accumulated juices, then add the crushed peppercorns, paprika, ginger, and chillies if using. Cook for 2 minutes, stirring all the time. Stir in the tomatoes and cook for a few minutes until they start to disintegrate.

7. Add the yogurt, a spoonful at a time, then season with salt to taste. Bring to the boil, stir, then lower the heat and cover the casserole with a tight-fitting lid (see note). Bake in the oven for about 1½-2 hours, until tender. If the meat is not tender after 1½ hours but quite dry, add 150 ml (¼ pint) water and return to the oven for a further 30 minutes. Serve with a rice pilaf and accompaniments of your choice.

NOTE: To improve the seal if necessary, cover the casserole with a double thickness of foil before positioning lid.

TECHNIQUE

Put the tomatoes in a heatproof bowl and pour on sufficient boiling water to cover. Leave for about 1 minute until the skins 'pop'. Remove and peel away the skins.

LAMB WITH POTATO

Use waxy potatoes for this dish and don't cut them into small pieces or they will disintegrate during cooking. Serve topped with raita or yogurt, and a little shredded chilli if you like. Basmati rice cooked with a handful of green lentils and tossed with chopped mint and crushed pepper is the ideal accompaniment.

SERVES 4-6

1 large onion
3 garlic cloves
2.5 cm (1 inch) piece fresh
    root ginger
1-2 hot red chillies
45 ml (3 tbsp) desiccated
    coconut
900 g (2 lb) lean boneless
    lamb
575 g (1¼ lb) waxy potatoes
45 ml (3 tbsp) ghee or
    vegetable oil
10 ml (2 tsp) paprika
5 ml (1 tsp) ground
    fenugreek
5 ml (1 tsp) ground
    turmeric
10 ml (2 tsp) ground
    coriander
5 ml (1 tsp) ground cumin
150 ml (¼ pint) yogurt
300 ml (½ pint) meat or
    vegetable stock
salt and pepper
TO SERVE
yogurt or raita
chillies, seeded (optional)

PREPARATION TIME
20 minutes
COOKING TIME
1½ hours
FREEZING
Suitable

680-450 CALS PER SERVING

1. Preheat the oven to 180°C (350°F) Mark 4. Peel and quarter the onion. Peel the garlic. Peel and roughly chop the ginger. Chop the chillies, discarding the seeds if a milder flavour is preferred. Put the onion, garlic, ginger, chillies and coconut in a blender with 30 ml (2 tbsp) water and process until smooth.

2. Trim the meat of any excess fat and cut into 4 cm (1½ inch) cubes. Peel the potatoes and cut into large chunks.

3. Heat the ghee or oil in a flameproof casserole, add the onion paste and cook until golden brown, stirring all the time. Add the spices and cook, stirring, over a high heat for 2 minutes.

4. Brown the meat and potatoes in the casserole over a high heat, in batches if necessary, turning constantly until thoroughly browned on all sides. Lower the heat and return all the meat and potatoes to the casserole. Add the yogurt, a spoonful at a time, stirring after each addition.

5. Add the stock and season liberally with salt. Bring to the boil, then reduce the heat, cover and cook in the oven for about 2 hours or until the meat is very tender.

6. When the meat and potatoes are tender, remove with a slotted spoon; set aside. Bring the sauce to the boil and boil steadily until the sauce is well reduced and very thick. Return the meat and potatoes to the casserole and stir to coat with the sauce. Serve topped with raita or yogurt, and shredded chillies if desired.

NOTE: If you're not certain that the potatoes you are using are waxy, add them to the casserole after 30 minutes of the cooking time.

VARIATION

Cook in a heavy-based pan or flameproof casserole at a gentle simmer on the hob for 1½ hours, rather than use the oven.

TECHNIQUE

Add the yogurt a spoonful at a time, stirring thoroughly after each addition.

LAMB TIKKA

These succulent meat skewers are served with a rich, nutty cream-based sauce. The sauce is improved if allowed to infuse for a while, so if you're marinating the meat overnight make the sauce the day before too. Serve the kebabs on shop-bought naan bread, with fresh coriander chutney (see page 72). Alternatively, simply accompany with an Indian *salat* of thinly sliced onions, radishes, tomatoes and chillies.

SERVES 4-6

900 g (2 lb) lean boneless lamb
1 medium onion
2 garlic cloves
7.5 cm (3 inch) piece fresh root ginger
5 ml (1 tsp) ground cumin
5 ml (1 tsp) ground turmeric
5 ml (1 tsp) cayenne pepper (optional)
30 ml (2 tbsp) finely chopped fresh coriander
60 ml (4 tbsp) thick yogurt
5 ml (1 tsp) salt
melted ghee, butter or vegetable oil, for brushing
SAUCE
2.5 ml (½ tsp) saffron strands
25 g (1 oz) blanched almonds
25 g (1 oz) shelled unsalted pistachio nuts
200 ml (7 fl oz) double cream
15 ml (1 tbsp) ghee or vegetable oil
seeds of 3 cardamoms
salt
150 ml (¼ pint) yogurt
TO FINISH
juice of ½ lemon
5 ml (1 tsp) garam masala

PREPARATION TIME
20 minutes, plus marinating
COOKING TIME About 30 minutes
FREEZING Not suitable

810-540 CALS PER SERVING

1. Trim the meat of excess fat, then cut into large cubes and place in a large non-metallic bowl.

2. Peel and finely chop the onion, garlic and ginger. Add to the lamb.

3. Add the cumin, turmeric, cayenne if using, chopped coriander, yogurt and salt. Toss thoroughly, so that each piece of meat is thoroughly coated with the spicy yogurt mixture. Cover the bowl and leave to marinate at cool room temperature for about 1 hour, or preferably overnight in the refrigerator (see note).

4. Meanwhile, make the sauce. Put the saffron in a bowl with 30 ml (2 tbsp) boiling water and leave to soak.

5. Put the almonds and pistachio nuts in a blender or food processor and work until finely chopped. Add half of the cream and process again until the mixture is smooth.

6. Heat the ghee or oil in a heavy-based pan. Add the nut mixture, together with the saffron, the remaining cream, cardamom seeds and salt to taste. Bring to

the boil, stirring. Simmer gently for about 5 minutes, stirring all the time. Remove from the heat and stir in the yogurt. Leave the sauce to stand for at least 30 minutes, or preferably overnight.

7. Preheat the grill (or barbecue). Thread the lamb onto kebab skewers. Place on the grill rack and cook under a moderately high heat for 15-25 minutes, turning occasionally, until evenly browned and cooked through. Brush with melted ghee, butter or oil during cooking.

8. Transfer the lamb to a warmed serving platter and sprinkle with the lemon juice and garam masala. Gently reheat the sauce and serve with the lamb.

NOTE: If you haven't time to marinate the meat overnight, use lamb fillet rather than leg to ensure a tender result.

TECHNIQUE

Thread the marinated meat onto kebab skewers and place on the grill rack.

LAMB PASANDA

This deliciously rich creamy curry is thickened with ground nuts and cream. It is important to ensure that the meat, nuts and onions are thoroughly browned, or the sauce will have an insipid colour. As this dish is very rich, it is best served with plain boiled rice and a simple vegetable accompaniment.

SERVES 4

50 g (2 oz) blanched
   almonds
50 g (2 oz) unsalted cashew
   nuts
30 ml (2 tbsp) sesame seeds
2.5 cm (1 inch) piece fresh
   root ginger
2 garlic cloves
2 onions
30 ml (2 tbsp) ghee or
   vegetable oil
10 ml (2 tsp) ground cumin
10 ml (2 tsp) ground
   coriander
2.5 ml (½ tsp) ground
   turmeric
2.5 ml (½ tsp) ground
   cardamom
2.5 ml (½ tsp) ground cloves
750 g (1½ lb) lean boneless
   lamb, cubed
150 ml (¼ pint) double
   cream
150 ml (¼ pint) coconut
   milk
30 ml (2 tbsp) lemon juice
salt

PREPARATION TIME
20 minutes
COOKING TIME
1½ hours
FREEZING
Suitable

865 CALS PER SERVING

1. Put the nuts in a heavy-based frying pan and dry-fry over a gentle heat until just golden brown. Remove from the pan and leave to cool. Toast the sesame seeds in the same way; allow to cool.

2. Peel and roughly chop the ginger. Peel the garlic. Peel and thinly slice the onions.

3. Tip the nuts into a blender or food processor and process briefly until finely chopped. Add the sesame seeds, ginger, garlic and 15 ml (1 tbsp) water and work to a purée.

4. Heat the ghee or oil in a large saucepan or flameproof casserole, add the onions and cook over a fairly high heat until tinged with brown. Add the nut mixture and cook over a moderately high heat for 2 minutes.

5. Add the ground spices and cook, stirring, for 2 minutes. Add the meat and cook over a high heat, turning constantly until browned and sealed on all sides.

6. Add the cream, coconut milk and 150 ml (¼ pint) water. Stir in the lemon juice and season with salt to taste. Bring slowly to the boil, then lower the heat and simmer very gently for about 1½ hours or until the lamb is tender. Serve with rice.

VARIATIONS

• Replace the lamb with beef. Use lean braising steak and cook for about 2 hours.
• Use chicken instead of lamb. Either joint a 1.4 kg (3 lb) chicken or use 4 chicken quarters, halved. Cook as above for about 45 minutes.

TECHNIQUE

Dry-fry the almonds and cashew nuts in a heavy-based frying pan over a low heat until tinged golden brown.

PORK VINDALOO

Vindaloo originates from the South of India and is meant to be slightly sour and very hot. Don't stint on the chillies – if yours are mild add more! In the Christian Indian community vindaloo is often made with pork. Muslims and Hindus, who do not eat pork, make it with mutton or beef. Serve this vindaloo with fluffy white basmati rice and cooling lassi or lager.

SERVES 4-6

900 g (2 lb) lean shoulder of pork

225 g (8 oz) onions (preferably red)

60 ml (4 tbsp) ghee or vegetable oil

6 garlic cloves

2.5 cm (1 inch) piece fresh root ginger

4-6 dried hot red chillies

10 ml (2 tsp) cumin seeds

10 ml (2 tsp) coriander seeds

10 ml (2 tsp) fenugreek seeds

10 ml (2 tsp) black peppercorns

5 ml (1 tsp) ground turmeric

10 ml (2 tsp) sugar

5 ml (1 tsp) salt

60 ml (4 tbsp) wine vinegar

8 green cardamoms

1 cinnamon stick

30 ml (2 tbsp) tomato purée

6 ripe juicy tomatoes

PREPARATION TIME
20 minutes
COOKING TIME
About 2 hours
FREEZING
Suitable

475-315 CALS PER SERVING

1. Trim the pork of excess fat and cut into 4 cm (1½ inch) cubes. Set aside while making the vindaloo paste.

2. To make the vindaloo paste, peel and chop the onions. Heat 30 ml (2 tbsp) of the ghee or oil in a frying pan. Add the onions and cook over a fairly high heat until golden brown, stirring all the time. Remove from the pan with a slotted spoon and drain on kitchen paper.

3. Peel the garlic and ginger and put into a blender or food processor with the onions and spices, except the cardamoms, cinnamon and 1 or 2 of the chillies. Add the sugar, salt and vinegar, then process until smooth. Mix with the cardamoms and cinnamon.

4. Heat the remaining 30 ml (2 tbsp) ghee or vegetable oil in a large heavy-based saucepan or flameproof casserole. Quickly fry the pork in batches turning constantly, until sealed and browned on all sides. Add the vindaloo paste and stir to ensure that the pork is evenly coated. Cook over a fairly high heat for about 5 minutes, stirring occasionally.

5. Roughly chop the tomatoes and add to the pan with the tomato purée, remaining chillies and 600 ml (1 pint) water. Bring to the boil, stirring, then lower the heat. Cover and simmer gently for about 1½ hours or until the pork

is very tender. Check from time to time to make sure that the sauce hasn't evaporated completely; if it looks too dry add a little more water.

6. If the sauce is too thin once the pork is cooked, cook over a high heat for a few minutes to boil off some of the liquid. Check the seasoning, adding a little more salt if necessary. Serve with rice.

VARIATIONS

• Replace the pork with lean boneless lamb.
• Use braising or stewing beef instead of pork.

TECHNIQUE

Add the vindaloo paste to the pork and stir to make sure the cubes of meat are coated on all sides.

MIXED VEGETABLES WITH COCONUT

Using fresh coconut is more time-consuming than opting for one of its processed forms but it makes a sauce with a superior texture and flavour. The technique suggested below for cracking a coconut is the quick way – be prepared for the milk to spill out! If you would prefer to catch it, pierce the 'eyes' with a screwdriver and drain the milk before you crack open the coconut.

SERVES 4

1 small or medium coconut
2 medium onions
2 garlic cloves
2.5 cm (1 inch) piece fresh
  root ginger
1 hot green chilli (optional)
5 ml (1 tsp) ground
  turmeric
10 ml (2 tsp) ground
  coriander
10 ml (2 tsp) coriander
  seeds
30 ml (2 tbsp) ghee or oil
2 large green peppers
2 carrots
8 spring onions
125 g (4 oz) green beans
salt and pepper
chopped fresh coriander, to
  garnish (optional)

PREPARATION TIME
30 minutes
COOKING TIME
30 minutes
FREEZING
Not suitable

395 CALS PER SERVING

1. Wrap the coconut in a tea-towel, grip it firmly and crack with a hammer. Remove the coconut flesh and peel off the hard brown skin, using a potato peeler or sharp knife. You will need about 225 g (8 oz) coconut flesh (use the rest for another dish). Roughly chop the flesh then drop it into a blender or food processor and work until very finely chopped. Add 150 ml (¼ pint) cold water and process again. Transfer the mixture from the blender to a bowl and set aside.

2. Peel and quarter the onions. Peel and halve the garlic cloves. Peel and roughly chop the ginger. Chop the chilli, if using, discarding the seeds if a milder flavour is preferred. Add the onions, garlic, ginger, chilli if using, turmeric, ground coriander and coriander seeds to the blender and process until finely chopped. Add a spoonful of water and process again to make a smooth purée.

3. Heat the ghee or oil in a large saucepan, add the onion and spice mixture and cook over a moderate heat, stirring for about 10 minutes until soft and golden brown.

4. Meanwhile, halve, core, deseed and roughly chop the peppers. Peel and slice the carrots. Trim and halve the spring onions. Trim the green beans.

5. Add the prepared vegetables to the pan and stir to coat in the onion and spice mixture. Add the coconut and season with salt and pepper to taste. Bring to the boil, then lower the heat. Cover and simmer very gently for about 20 minutes or until the vegetables are just tender. Check the pan from time to time to make sure that the vegetables are still moist; if they look dry, add a little extra water.

6. Serve sprinkled with chopped coriander if desired.

TECHNIQUE

Peel off the hard brown skin from the coconut flesh, using a vegetable peeler.

OKRA WITH ONION AND TOMATO

This makes a tasty side dish to serve with plain grilled fish or meat. The quantity of masala spice mix is more than you need for this recipe, but it can be stored in an airtight jar and used as required. If you're short of time you could omit the spice mix and simply serve the okra sprinkled with the crisp onions.

SERVES 4

2 medium onions
45 ml (3 tbsp) ghee or
   vegetable oil
2 garlic cloves
2.5 cm (1 inch) piece fresh
   root ginger
1 hot chilli (optional)
3 tomatoes
450 g (1 lb) okra
10 ml (2 tsp) ground
   coriander
2.5 ml (½ tsp) turmeric
2.5 ml (½ tsp) ground
   cinnamon
salt and pepper
30 ml (2 tbsp) thick yogurt
30 ml (2 tbsp) chopped fresh
   coriander

MASALA SPICE MIX

15 ml (1 tbsp) coriander
   seeds
15 ml (1 tbsp) cumin seeds
10 ml (2 tsp) black
   peppercorns
3 dried red chillies

PREPARATION TIME
20 minutes
COOKING TIME
25 minutes
FREEZING Not suitable

175 CALS PER SERVING

1. First make the masala spice mix. Dry-fry the spices in a small frying pan for about 3 minutes until they begin to pop and release their aroma; stir frequently to ensure that they don't burn. Let cool slightly, then grind using a pestle and mortar. Store in an airtight jar until required.

2. Peel the onions. Halve and thinly slice one onion; quarter the other. Heat the ghee or oil in a frying pan, add the sliced onion and cook over a medium heat for about 10 minutes until dark golden brown and crisp. Drain on kitchen paper and set aside. Reserve the oil in the pan.

3. Peel and roughly chop the garlic and ginger. Slice the chilli, discarding the seeds if a milder flavour is preferred. Skin the tomatoes if preferred, then chop the flesh. Trim the okra.

4. Put the quartered onion, garlic and ginger in a blender with 15 ml (1 tbsp) water and process until smooth. Add the spices and process again.

5. Reheat the ghee or oil remaining in the frying pan, add the onion paste and cook over a high heat for 2 minutes, stirring all the time. Lower the heat and cook for 5 minutes or until the onion paste is golden brown and softened.

6. Add the chopped tomatoes with the chilli if using. Season with salt and pepper to taste. Cook for 5 minutes until the tomato has reduced down, then add the okra and stir to coat in the mixture. Cover and simmer gently for about 5 minutes until the okra is just tender.

7. Stir in the yogurt, a spoonful at a time, then add the coriander and heat through gently. Transfer to a serving dish and sprinkle with the crisp onions and a little of the masala spice mix to serve.

TECHNIQUE

Trim the okra, removing a small piece from each end. Do not cut into the flesh, or the dish will acquire an unpleasant glutinous texture during cooking.

MATTAR PANEER

Paneer is a kind of curd cheese that's really easy to make at home. It's a good idea to make it the day before you intend to serve this dish, as the paneer needs to be pressed for about 4 hours to make it firm enough to cut. Once pressed, it can be kept in the refrigerator for up to 4 days.

SERVES 4

2.3 litres (4 pints) full-fat milk

about 75 ml (5 tbsp) strained lemon juice

1 medium onion

5 cm (2 inch) piece fresh root ginger

450 g (1 lb) fresh ripe tomatoes

45 ml (3 tbsp) ghee or vegetable oil

5 ml (1 tsp) ground turmeric

5 ml (1 tsp) ground coriander

5 ml (1 tsp) cumin seeds

2.5-5 ml (½-1 tsp) cayenne pepper

350 g (12 oz) shelled fresh or frozen peas (see note)

5 ml (1 tsp) sugar

salt and pepper

30 ml (2 tbsp) chopped fresh coriander

15 ml (1 tbsp) chopped fresh mint (optional)

garam masala, to taste

PREPARATION TIME
20-30 minutes, plus pressing
COOKING TIME
20 minutes
FREEZING
Suitable

375 CALS PER SERVING

1. To make the paneer, bring the milk to the boil in a deep saucepan. As soon as it boils, remove from the heat and add the lemon juice, all at once. Stir thoroughly, then return to the heat for about 1 minute; the curds and whey should separate very quickly. Immediately remove the pan from the heat. If they don't separate, add another 15 ml (1 tbsp) lemon juice and repeat.

2. Line a large sieve or colander with a double thickness of muslin or cheesecloth and place over a large bowl. Pour the curds and whey into the lined sieve or colander and leave to drain and cool slightly.

3. When the muslin is cool enough to handle, gather it up around the curds and squeeze to remove excess whey. Reserve 120 ml (4 fl oz) of the whey and keep, covered, in the refrigerator; discard the rest.

4. Wrap the cheesecloth tightly around the curds, then place on a chopping board. Put a second board on top and weigh it down with a few large cans or weights. Leave undisturbed for about 4 hours, or until the cheese feels firm to the touch.

5. When ready, cut the paneer cheese into small cubes. Peel and chop the onion and ginger. Skin the tomatoes if preferred, then chop the flesh.

6. Heat the ghee or oil in a large frying pan. Add the paneer and cook until golden brown on all sides; remove from the pan with a slotted spoon and set aside. Add the onion and ginger to the pan and cook over a medium heat until the onion is golden brown. Add the spices and cook for 2 minutes, stirring all the time. Add the tomatoes and the reserved whey and bring to the boil. Simmer for 2-3 minutes, then add the peas, with the cheese, sugar and salt and pepper to taste.

7. Cover and simmer gently for about 15 minutes or until the peas are tender. Stir in the coriander and mint if using. Sprinkle with garam masala before serving, garnished with mint and/or coriander.

NOTE: If using fresh peas, you will need to buy about 900 g (2 lb) in pods.

TECHNIQUE

Gather the muslin up around the curds and squeeze to remove excess whey.

SPICED POTATOES AND CAULIFLOWER

Everyone's favourite vegetable curry, this combination of cauliflower and potato, known as *aloo gobi*, makes a delicious side dish. Alternatively, it can be served as a vegetarian main dish, but you may wish to double the quantities. If serving as an accompaniment to a very hot dish, you might prefer a milder creamy version (see variation).

SERVES 4

450 g (1 lb) waxy potatoes
450 g (1 lb) cauliflower
    florets
1 medium onion
5 cm (2 inch) piece fresh
    root ginger
1 hot green chilli
60 ml (4 tbsp) ghee or
    vegetable oil
5 ml (1 tsp) black mustard
    seeds
5 ml (1 tsp) cumin seeds
5 ml (1 tsp) ground cumin
2.5 ml (½ tsp) ground
    turmeric
salt and pepper

PREPARATION TIME
15 minutes
COOKING TIME
15 minutes
FREEZING
Not suitable

270 CALS PER SERVING

1. Peel the potatoes and cut into large chunks. Place in a saucepan with enough salted water to cover, bring to the boil and boil for 5 minutes. Drain.

2. Meanwhile, cut the cauliflower into smaller florets if necessary. Peel and finely chop the onion and ginger. Finely slice the chilli, discarding the seeds if a milder flavour is preferred.

3. Heat the ghee or oil in a large frying pan. Add the onion and ginger and cook over a medium heat until the onion is golden brown but not burnt. Add the chilli and spices and cook for 2 minutes, stirring all the time.

4. Add the potatoes and cauliflower, stirring to coat them in the spice mixture. Season with salt and pepper and stir in 45 ml (3 tbsp) water. Cover with a lid and cook gently over a medium heat for about 10 minutes or until the potatoes and cauliflower are tender. Check the pan occasionally during cooking, adding a little extra water if necessary to prevent sticking. Don't overcook the vegetables; they should retain their shape.

VARIATION

For a milder, creamier version, omit the chilli and replace the water with 150 ml (¼ pint) coconut milk.

TECHNIQUE

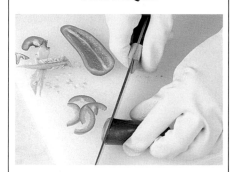

Wearing rubber gloves to prevent skin irritation, halve the chilli and cut into very thin slices, removing the seeds for a milder flavour.

AUBERGINE BHAJI

For this recipe it really is advantageous to degorge the aubergines before cooking. These days most aubergines are not bitter, but they do soak up copious amounts of oil during cooking, and degorging can considerably reduce this. An excellent accompaniment to all kinds of Indian dishes, this bhaji is particularly good served as part of a vegetarian meal.

SERVES 4

2 medium aubergines
salt
1 large onion
2 garlic cloves
2.5 cm (1 inch) piece fresh
   root ginger
large handful of fresh
   coriander
about 75 ml (5 tbsp) ghee or
   vegetable oil
15 ml (1 tbsp) coriander
   seeds
15 ml (1 tbsp) mustard
   seeds
15 ml (1 tbsp) poppy seeds
5 ml (1 tsp) cumin seeds
1 tomato, skinned if
   preferred
10 ml (2 tsp) red wine
   vinegar

PREPARATION TIME
15 minutes, plus degorging
COOKING TIME
About 25 minutes
FREEZING
Not suitable

215 CALS PER SERVING

1. Trim the aubergines and cut into fairly thick slices. Halve each slice or cut into thirds. Layer the aubergine in a colander, sprinkling each layer generously with salt. Put a plate on top to weight down and leave to degorge for at least 30 minutes.

2. Peel and quarter the onion. Peel and halve the garlic. Peel and roughly chop the ginger. Trim the coriander and roughly chop.

3. Put the onion, garlic, ginger, coriander and a spoonful of water in a blender and process until smooth.

4. Rinse the aubergines under cold running water to remove all traces of salt. Drain and pat dry thoroughly with kitchen paper.

5. Heat the ghee or oil in a large frying pan or wok. Add the onion mixture and cook, stirring, for 5 minutes, until golden brown. Add the spices and cook for 2 minutes, stirring all the time.

6. Add the aubergines and turn to coat in the spice mixture (see note). Cook over a high heat, turning frequently, until they are just tinged with brown and coated in the spice mixture.

7. Chop the tomato and add to the pan with 30 ml (2 tbsp) water. Lower the heat and simmer for about 15 minutes or until the aubergines are just tender but still retain their shape. Add the vinegar and salt and pepper to taste. Serve immediately.

NOTE: Unless your wok or frying pan is very large, you will need to fry the aubergines in 2 or 3 batches, adding a little more ghee or oil to the pan as necessary. Once browned, return them all to the pan.

VARIATION

Enrich the sauce with 60 ml (4 tbsp) thick yogurt. Stir in, a tablespoon at a time, after adding the tomato. Omit the water and vinegar.

TECHNIQUE

Stack a few aubergine slices on top of one another, then cut down to slice each round into three.

VEGETABLE BIRYANI

In India biryani is traditionally served at festivals and other celebrations, and looking at the extensive list of ingredients, you can see why! It is most often made with chunks of lamb but this vegetarian version is just as spectacular. Make it on a day when you can set aside plenty of time for cooking. Serve biryani as a meal in itself, accompanied by a dal dish and plenty of chutneys.

SERVES 4

1 large onion
3 garlic cloves
225 g (8 oz) waxy potatoes
125 g (4 oz) French beans
2 carrots
225 g (8 oz) cauliflower
    florets
350 g (12 oz) basmati rice
about 60 ml (4 tbsp) ghee or
    vegetable oil
25 g (1 oz) shelled unsalted
    pistachio nuts
25 g (1 oz) slivered blanched
    almonds
25 g (1 oz) raisins
2 large pinches of saffron
1 cinnamon stick
6 black peppercorns
6 cloves
4 cardamoms
5 ml (1 tsp) ground cumin
5 ml (1 tsp) cayenne pepper
75 g (3 oz) shelled peas
150 ml (¼ pint) thick yogurt
TO SERVE
hard-boiled eggs (optional)
garam masala

PREPARATION TIME
25 minutes
COOKING TIME
40 minutes
FREEZING Not suitable

670 CALS PER SERVING

1. Peel and halve the onion, then cut into very thin semi-circular slices. Peel and crush the garlic. Peel the potatoes and cut into chunks. Trim and halve the beans. Peel and slice the carrots. Break the cauliflower into small florets. Wash the rice in a sieve under cold running water; drain.

2. Heat the ghee or oil in a heavy-based saucepan or flameproof casserole. Add the onion and cook over a high heat for about 5 minutes or until golden brown. Remove from the pan with a slotted spoon and drain on kitchen paper; set aside.

3. Add the nuts and raisins to the ghee or oil remaining in the pan and cook for 1 minute, or until the nuts are lightly browned. Remove from the pan with a slotted spoon and drain on kitchen paper; set aside.

4. Add the spices and garlic to the pan, adding a little extra ghee or oil to the pan if necessary. Add the prepared vegetables and the peas and cook, stirring for 2 minutes. Add the yogurt, a spoonful at a time, stirring thoroughly after each addition. Add 60 ml (4 tbsp) water, cover with a lid and simmer for 10 minutes or until the vegetables are just tender.

5. Meanwhile, put the rice in another saucepan with 600 ml (1 pint) water and salt to taste. Bring quickly to the boil, then lower the heat, partially cover with a lid and simmer for 10 minutes or until just tender and the liquid is absorbed.

6. Add the rice to the vegetables, re-cover and simmer gently for 5-10 minutes or until the rice and vegetables are tender. Season with salt and pepper to taste. Pile onto a warmed serving platter and top with the nuts, raisins, fried onions and hard-boiled eggs if using. Sprinkle with garam masala to taste and serve immediately.

TECHNIQUE

Fry the nuts and raisins in the pan until lightly browned. Remove with a slotted spoon and drain on kitchen paper.

RICE AND DAL PILAU

Chana dal is a mustard yellow coloured dal that is sold hulled and split by Indian and Pakistani grocers. Here it is cooked with rice, nuts and sesame seeds to make a delicious and highly nutritious accompaniment. As it is packed with protein, this dish also makes a good basis for a vegetarian meal. Try serving it with a vegetable curry, a relish or *salat*, and a chutney or two.

SERVES 4-6

50 g (2 oz) chana dal
350 g (12 oz) basmati rice
1 medium onion
1-2 garlic cloves (optional)
1 hot green chilli, or 2 dried
    red chillies
60 ml (4 tbsp) ghee or
    vegetable oil
40 g (1½ oz) cashew nuts
10 ml (2 tsp) cumin seeds
4 pieces cassia bark, or
    1 cinnamon stick
1 bay leaf
600 ml (1 pint) vegetable
    stock
5 ml (1 tsp) salt, or to taste
15 ml (1 tbsp) toasted
    sesame seeds
large pinch of garam
    masala, to serve

PREPARATION TIME
About 15 minutes, plus soaking
COOKING TIME
30 minutes, plus 10 minutes
standing
FREEZING
Suitable

580-385 CALS PER SERVING

1. Pick over the dal, removing any small stones or green coloured pieces. Wash thoroughly under cold running water, then put in a bowl with plenty of cold water to cover and leave to soak for 3 hours.

2. Wash the rice in a sieve under cold running water, then put in a bowl and add plenty of cold water to cover. Leave to soak for 1 hour.

3. Peel and halve the onion, then cut into thin semi-circular slices. Peel and thinly slice the garlic. Slice the fresh green chilli, discarding the seeds if a milder flavour is preferred. If using dried chillies, leave whole.

4. Heat the ghee or oil in a large heavy-based saucepan or flameproof casserole. Add the cashew nuts and fry over a high heat until golden brown. Remove from the pan with a slotted spoon and drain on kitchen paper; set aside.

5. Add the onion and garlic to the pan and cook, stirring, until the onion is just tinged with brown. Add the chilli and spices and cook for 1 minute, stirring all the time. Lower the heat slightly. Thoroughly drain the dal and add to the pan. Add the stock and salt.

6. Quickly bring to the boil, stir with a fork, then cover with a tight-fitting lid.

Lower the heat and simmer for 10 minutes. Drain the rice and add to the pan; re-cover and cook for a further 10 minutes. Shake the pan occasionally as it cooks but resist the temptation to lift the lid or precious steam will escape and the rice is more likely to stick and burn on the base of the pan.

7. Switch off the heat and leave the pan undisturbed for 10 minutes. Turn the rice and dal onto a serving dish and fluff up the grains with a fork. Check the seasoning, adding a little extra salt if necessary. Sprinkle with the cashews, sesame seeds and garam masala before serving.

TECHNIQUE

Add the pre-soaked and thoroughly drained dal to the fried onion and spice mixture.

LEMON DAL

Masoor dal is the common red split lentil or Egyptian lentil that is widely available from supermarkets. Really salmon rather than red in colour, these lentils cook quickly and do not require pre-soaking. Here they are combined with turmeric and lemon to make a comforting 'wet' dal that will complement most curries. For a mildly spiced flavour, omit the chilli.

SERVES 4-6

1 medium onion
1 garlic clove (optional)
1 hot green chilli (optional)
60 ml (4 tbsp) ghee or
    vegetable oil
2.5 ml (½ tsp) ground
    turmeric
225 g (8 oz) masoor dal (red
    split lentils)
5 ml (1 tsp) salt, or to taste
finely grated rind and juice
    of 1 lemon
5 ml (1 tsp) masala spice
    mix (page 52), or cumin
    seeds

PREPARATION TIME
10 minutes
COOKING TIME
30 minutes
FREEZING
Suitable

325-215 CALS PER SERVING

1. Peel and halve the onion, then cut into very thin semi-circular slices. Peel and crush the garlic, if using. Chop the chilli if using, discarding the seeds if a milder flavour is preferred.

2. Heat half of the ghee or oil in a heavy-based saucepan or casserole. Add the onion and cook over a high heat for about 5 minutes or until golden brown. Remove from the pan with a slotted spoon and drain on kitchen paper.

3. Add the turmeric to the ghee or oil remaining in the pan and cook, stirring, for 1 minute. Add the dal, salt, and the lemon rind and juice. Cook, stirring, for 1 minute, then add 300 ml (½ pint) water.

4. Bring quickly to the boil, cover with a tight-fitting lid, then turn the heat to its lowest setting and cook for 25-30 minutes. Resist the temptation to lift the lid as the dal cooks or precious steam will be lost and the dal will stick and burn on the base of the pan. When cooked, the dal should be very soft and all the water absorbed.

5. When the dal is almost ready, heat the remaining ghee or oil in a small pan. Add the masala spice mix or cumin seeds, the garlic and chilli if using; cook, stirring, for 2 minutes.

6. Beat the dal with a wooden spoon to a fairly smooth, moist consistency. If it is too dry add a spoonful of hot water; if too moist, cook, stirring, over a high heat to evaporate excess moisture. Check the seasoning, adding a little more salt if necessary.

7. Turn the dal into a warmed serving dish. Pour over the hot ghee mixture and scatter the fried onions on top. Serve immediately.

TECHNIQUE

Beat the dal with a wooden spoon, to give a fairly smooth, moist consistency.

CHICK PEAS WITH SPINACH

This accompaniment goes well with most meat curries. It is also excellent with Spiced Fried Fish (page 28). For a quick supper dish to serve 4 as a meal in itself, use canned rather than fresh chick peas.

SERVES 4-6

225 g (8 oz) dried chick
    peas, or two 425 g (15 oz)
    cans
5 ml (1 tsp) salt, or to taste
2.5 cm (1 inch) piece fresh
    root ginger
3 garlic cloves
4 tomatoes
450 g (1 lb) spinach leaves
45 ml (3 tbsp) ghee or
    vegetable oil
10 ml (2 tsp) ground
    coriander
5 ml (1 tsp) ground cumin
10 ml (2 tsp) paprika
handful of fresh coriander,
    roughly torn
black pepper
coriander sprigs, to garnish

PREPARATION TIME
10 minutes, plus overnight
soaking for dried chick peas
COOKING TIME
2¼ - 3¼ hours, or 15 minutes if
using canned chick peas
FREEZING
Suitable

325-215 CALS PER SERVING

1. Pick over the dried chick peas if using, discarding any small stones or shrivelled peas. Rinse thoroughly in plenty of cold running water, then put into a bowl and add plenty of cold water to cover. Leave to soak overnight.

2. Drain the dried chick peas, put them in a large saucepan with plenty of water and bring to the boil. Lower the heat and simmer gently for 2-3 hours or until tender, adding salt towards the end of the cooking time. Drain well. If using canned chick peas, simply drain and rinse under cold running water.

3. Peel and finely chop the ginger. Peel and crush the garlic. Immerse the tomatoes in boiling water for 30 seconds, then remove and peel away the skins. Finely chop the tomato flesh. Trim and chop the spinach.

4. Heat the ghee or oil in a large heavy-based saucepan or casserole. Add the ginger, garlic and spices and cook for 2 minutes, stirring all the time. Add the chick peas and stir to coat in the spice mixture.

5. Add the tomatoes, torn coriander and spinach. Cook for 2 minutes, then cover with a lid and simmer gently for 10 minutes. Season with salt and pepper before serving, garnished with coriander.

NOTE: The cooking time for dried chick peas will depend on their 'freshness'. If they have been stored for a long time and look shrivelled, they may take even longer than 3 hours to cook.

VARIATION

Use another pulse in place of the chick peas. Black eye beans are particularly good; cook as above.

TECHNIQUE

Add the chick peas to the pan and stir to coat in the spice mixture.

SPINACH PARATHAS

These tasty breads are best served warm from the oven. However, they can be made in advance, then later sprinkled with a little water, wrapped in foil and reheated in a warm oven.

DOUGH
175 g (6 oz) plain wholemeal flour
175 g (6 oz) plain white flour
salt and pepper
25 g (1 oz) butter
FILLING
1 garlic clove
1 red or green chilli
125 g (4 oz) spinach leaves
15 ml (1 tbsp) vegetable oil
5 ml (1 tsp) cumin seeds
30 ml (2 tbsp) chopped fresh coriander
ghee, butter or vegetable oil, for brushing

PREPARATION TIME
30 minutes, plus resting
COOKING TIME
About 10 minutes per paratha
FREEZING
Suitable

1. Put the flours in a food processor with 5 ml (1 tsp) salt and the butter; work until butter is finely chopped. Measure 300 ml (½ pint) water. With the machine running, pour half the water through the feeder tube and process for 2 minutes.

2. Now with the machine still running, slowly add enough of the remaining water to make a dough. As soon as the mixture comes together in a ball, stop the machine. You may not need to add all of the water; the amount required depends on the absorbency of the flour.

3. Knead the dough on a floured surface for 10 minutes until smooth, soft and pliable, but not sticky. Shape into a ball, cover with cling film and leave to rest for 30 minutes.

4. Meanwhile, make the filling. Peel and crush the garlic. Chop the chilli, discarding the seeds if a milder flavour is preferred. Trim the spinach and chop roughly.

5. Heat the oil in a frying pan, add the chilli and garlic and cook for 2 minutes. Add the cumin seeds and cook for a further 1 minute. Add the spinach and cook until just wilted. Remove from the heat, add the coriander and season with salt and pepper to taste. Leave to cool.

6. Divide the dough into 12 pieces. Cover all but one with cling film. Roll this piece into a 20 cm (8 inch) circle. Using a slotted spoon, place a little spinach mixture in the middle of the circle.

7. Gather up the edges of the dough over the filling and twist to seal. Sprinkle with a little flour, then carefully flatten the ball and roll it out to a 15 cm (6 inch) circle; cover with cling film and set aside. Repeat with the remaining dough and filling.

8. Heat a griddle or heavy-based frying pan until it is very hot. Add 1 paratha, cook over a high heat for 1 minute, then lower the heat and cook more gently for 2 minutes or until small bubbles appear on the surface and the underside is golden brown in patches. Turn the paratha over and cook the second side in the same way.

9. Brush the top with a little melted ghee or butter, turn the paratha again and cook for 1 minute. Brush again, turn and cook for 1 minute or until crisp on the outside and cooked right through. Wrap in foil and keep warm while cooking the remainder. Serve warm.

TECHNIQUE

Gather the edges of the dough up over the filling and twist together to seal.

POORIS

These spectacular puffed-up breads are fun to make, and are at their best served straight from the pan while still hot and puffed up. If yours have deflated by the time you serve them, try reviving them by placing under a hot grill for a few seconds.

MAKES 6

175 g (6 oz) plain wholemeal
    flour
5 ml (1 tsp) salt
vegetable oil for deep-frying

PREPARATION TIME
15 minutes, plus resting
COOKING TIME
About 10 minutes
FREEZING
Not suitable

200 CALS PER POORI

1. Put the flour and salt in a food processor and process briefly to mix. Measure 150 ml (¼ pint) cold water in a jug. With the machine running, gradually add half of the water through the feeder tube.

2. Now with the machine still running, slowly add enough of the remaining water to make a dough. As soon as the mixture comes together in a ball, stop the machine. You may not need to add all of the water, the amount required depends on the absorbency of the flour.

3. Turn the dough onto a floured surface and knead for 10 minutes until it is smooth, soft and pliable but not sticky. Shape the dough into a ball, cover with cling film and leave to rest at room temperature for 30 minutes.

4. Divide the dough into 6 equal pieces. Cover all except one with cling film. Roll this piece out to a 12 cm (5 inch) circle. Cover with cling film and set aside. Repeat with the remaining dough.

5. Heat the oil in a deep-fat fryer. Test the temperature by dropping in a small cube of bread – it should sizzle immediately on contact with the oil and rise to the surface; remove with a slotted spoon.

6. Carefully slide a poori into the hot oil and press it down to immerse; it should

puff up almost instantly. Turn it over to cook the second side, constantly moving the poori about with the spoon, until it is golden brown. Drain on kitchen paper and keep warm while you cook the remainder. Serve warm.

TECHNIQUE

Using the back of a metal spoon, keep the poori immersed in the hot oil as it cooks.

FRESH CORIANDER CHUTNEY

This fresh-tasting cross between a relish, chutney and a dip goes well with all Indian rice dishes and breads. It will also enliven plain grilled chicken or fish, and adds flavour to salad dressings too. Make the chutney as hot or as mild as you like, by increasing or reducing the amount of chillies. It will keep in the refrigerator for up to 1 week.

SERVES 8

1 medium onion
1-2 garlic cloves
1-2 green chillies
1 large bunch fresh
   coriander
30 ml (2 tbsp) ground
   almonds
45 ml (3 tbsp) lime or lemon
   juice
45 ml (3 tbsp) vegetable oil
10 ml (2 tsp) sugar
5 ml (1 tsp) salt, or to taste
black pepper

PREPARATION TIME
10 minutes, plus standing
COOKING TIME
5 minutes
FREEZING
Suitable

85 CALS PER SERVING

1. Peel and quarter the onion. Peel the garlic. Chop the chillies, discarding the seeds if a milder flavour is preferred. Trim the roots from the coriander if attached, but leave some of the stalks. Wash and thoroughly dry if necessary. Chop roughly.

2. Line a grill pan with foil. Spread the ground almonds on the foil and toast under a medium-hot grill until lightly browned, shaking the pan occasionally so that they brown evenly. Do not let them burn or they will taste bitter. Leave to cool.

3. Put the onion, garlic, chillies, coriander and ground almonds in a blender or food processor, together with all of the other ingredients. Process in short bursts until the ingredients are well chopped and evenly mixed, but still retain some texture.

4. Turn into a bowl and leave at room temperature for at least 1 hour to let the flavours develop. Taste again and add a little more seasoning if necessary.

VARIATION

Fresh Mint Chutney: Use a large bunch of fresh mint instead of the coriander. Replace the almonds with sesame seeds. Add a little grated fresh root ginger and a little extra sugar, to taste.

TECHNIQUE

Scrape down the sides of the food processor or blender from time to time to ensure the ingredients are fairly evenly chopped.

COCONUT ICE CREAM

Coconuts are plentiful all over India and are used extensively in sweet and savoury dishes. Although this recipe isn't a true ice cream, it makes a simple refreshing dessert to follow a spicy main course. The edible rose petal decoration is optional, but provides a stunning contrast to the gleaming white ice cream.

SERVES 8

275 g (10 oz) granulated
  sugar
four 450 ml (¾ pint) cans
  coconut milk
TO DECORATE (optional)
few dark red rose petals
few shredded dried red rose
  petals
freshly grated nutmeg
ground cinnamon

PREPARATION TIME
15 minutes
COOKING TIME
10 minutes
FREEZING TIME
5 hours

800 CALS PER SERVING

1. Set the freezer to fast-freeze. Put the sugar and 600 ml (1 pint) water in a medium heavy-based saucepan and dissolve over a medium heat, stirring occasionally. As soon as it is dissolved, stop stirring, increase the heat and boil rapidly for 10 minutes to make a sugar syrup. Leave to cool completely.

2. Blend the cooled syrup with the coconut milk. Pour into a shallow freezerproof container, cover and freeze for about 3 hours or until partially frozen.

3. Spoon the mixture into a blender or food processor and quickly blend on high speed to break down the ice crystals without letting the ice cream melt. Immediately return to the container, re-cover and freeze again just until mushy. This will probably take another 2 hours.

4. Tip the ice cream into the blender or processor and process again as before. Return to the container, cover tightly and freeze for about 3 hours until firm. The ice cream is now ready to eat.

5. Remove the ice cream from the freezer and leave for 10-20 minutes at cool room temperature to soften before serving.

6. Scoop the ice cream into serving dishes. Scatter with the rose petals, nutmeg and cinnamon if using.

TECHNIQUE

Work the partially frozen ice cream in the food processor or blender to break down the ice crystals and ensure an even-textured result, without allowing the ice cream to melt.

KULFI

This is an extremely rich Indian ice cream, which is easy to make at home as it doesn't need to be churned or stirred during freezing. In India, kulfi is traditionally set in special cone-shaped containers. Clean empty yogurt pots are ideal substitutes, or you can use any small freezerproof containers, such as ramekins. I like to serve kulfi scattered with extra pistachios and sprinkled with icing sugar, grated chocolate or cocoa powder – not very authentic but delicious!

SERVES 4

450 ml (¾ pint) double
  cream
400 g (14 fl oz) can
  condensed milk
125 g (4 oz) caster sugar
few drops of green food
  colouring (optional)
few drops of almond
  essence
25 g (1 oz) shelled unsalted
  pistachio nuts
40 g (1½ oz) ground
  almonds
pistachio nuts, to decorate

PREPARATION TIME
10 minutes
COOKING TIME
25 minutes
FREEZING TIME
4 hours

1060 CALS PER SERVING

1. Set the freezer to fast-freeze. Put the cream, condensed milk and sugar in a large heavy-based, non-stick saucepan and heat gently, stirring all the time, until the sugar is completely dissolved.

2. Bring to the boil, stirring, then reduce the heat until the mixture is boiling steadily (see note). Cook, stirring occasionally, for about 15-20 minutes or until the mixture is thick enough to coat the back of a spoon and reduced to about 600 ml (1 pint); it should be yellow in colour.

3. In the meantime, finely chop the nuts.

4. When the mixture is cooked, colour it pale green with a few drops of green colouring if desired. Stir in the almond essence, pistachio nuts and ground almonds. Leave to cool slightly.

5. Divide the mixture between 4 individual moulds, about 150 ml (¼ pint) capacity. Leave to cool completely.

6. Stand the containers on a baking sheet or plate and place in the freezer for about 4 hours or until frozen.

7. To serve, run a knife around the edge of each kulfi to loosen, then invert onto individual serving plates. Scatter with pistachio nuts and serve immediately.

NOTE: Cook the mixture as rapidly as possible without boiling over. Watch carefully during cooking to ensure it doesn't boil over, or stick to the pan.

TECHNIQUE

Cook the mixture steadily until yellow in colour and thick enough to coat the back of a wooden spoon.

FRUIT SALAD

The best way to end a spicy meal is with a piece of refreshing fruit. If you're looking for something a little more sophisticated, try this tempting fruit salad – enhanced with a cardamom and mint scented syrup. Choose ripe fruit in optimum condition; under-ripe mangoes and pineapples are simply not worth eating. Pineapples should have a rich golden brown skin and a sweet aroma. Mangoes should give slightly when gently pressed. Include other exotic fruits, such as guavas, watermelon, lychees and rambutans, when available and as the mood takes you!

SERVES 6

50 g (2 oz) caster sugar
4 green cardamoms
6 large fresh mint sprigs
finely grated rind and juice
  of I lime
I ripe pineapple
I large ripe mango
3 small juicy oranges
I papaya

PREPARATION TIME
20 minutes, plus infusing and
chilling
COOKING TIME
5 minutes
FREEZING
Not suitable

125 CALS PER SERVING

1. Put the sugar in a small heavy-based pan with 200 ml (7 fl oz) water. Crush the cardamoms with a rolling pin to split the pods slightly. Crush 4 mint sprigs in the same way. Add the crushed mint and cardamoms to the pan.

2. Heat the mixture gently until the sugar dissolves, then bring to the boil and boil for I minute. Allow to cool and infuse for at least I hour or until completely cold. Discard the mint sprigs and cardamom pods.

3. Strip the leaves from the remaining mint sprigs and add them to the sugar syrup with the lime rind and juice. Pour into a bowl and chill while preparing the fruit.

4. Peel the pineapple, halve and discard the tough central core. Cut the flesh into large chunks. Cut the mango across either side of the stone, then cut the flesh into large slices and peel off the skin. Chop the flesh surrounding the stone.

5. Peel the oranges, then cut each one into wedges. Cut the papaya in half and scoop out the seeds with a teaspoon. Cut the flesh into slices and remove the skin.

6. Arrange the fruit in a shallow serving dish and pour over the syrup. Cover the bowl and chill in the refrigerator for 30 minutes before serving.

NOTE: Don't cut the fruit up too small; keep the pieces chunky and attractive. Include a wedge of watermelon and/or papaya if you like. Just remember to provide dessert forks and spoons!

TECHNIQUE

Peel the skin from the pineapple using a sharp knife, then remove any remaining brown 'eyes' with the tip of a knife.

Special ingredients can be obtained by mail order from:
THE CURRY DIRECTORY, P.O. Box 7, Liss, Hants, GU33 7YS; Tel: 01730 894949

If you would like further information about the **Good Housekeeping Cookery Club**, please write to:
Penny Smith, Ebury Press, Random House, 20 Vauxhall Bridge Road, London SW1V 2SA.